Simon Cheshire

Story illustrated by
Pet Gotohda

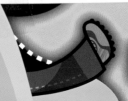

Heinemann

Before Reading

Find out about

- How hair grows
- Some of the different hairstyles people choose

Tricky words

- colours
- follicles
- palms
- soles
- melanin
- carotene
- extreme

Introduce these tricky words and help the reader when they come across them later!

Text starter

Hair grows out of follicles all over your body. Two things give hair its colour: melanin and carotene. Throughout history, people have liked different hairstyles just as they do today.

All about Hair

What part of your body does not hurt
if you cut it?
What part of your body comes in
lots of different colours? It's your hair!

Hair is made of dead skin cells!

Hair follicles

Hair grows out of tiny holes in your skin. The tiny holes are called follicles. If your follicles are round, your hair grows straight. If your follicles are flat, your hair grows curly.

Hair grows all over you, but many of the hairs are so tiny you can hardly see them.

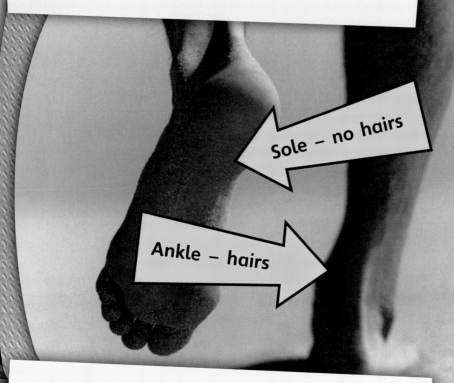

Sole – no hairs

Ankle – hairs

There are only two parts of your body where hair does not grow.
They are the palms of your hands and the soles of your feet.

Hair colour

There are lots of different hair colours.

Two things give hair its colour:

- melanin (which is dark)
- carotene (which is reddish-yellow).

All hair colour is a mix of these two. Old people go grey because their hair stops making melanin.

How hair grows

The hair on your head grows about two millimetres every week. It grows faster in warm weather! You have about 100,000 hairs on your head and you lose about 80 of them every day.

Hairy history

All through history, people have been very fussy about their hairstyles. The Romans brushed their hair every day but they only washed it once a year!

Would you wash your hair just once a year?

In the 18th century, wigs were very popular. Men and women often wore very tall wigs.

Why did people wear wigs? The wigs covered up the dirty, smelly hair that most people had because they did not wash it!

Hairstyles in history

Take a look at these hairstyles.

Would you like to have hair like **THIS**?

In the 1920s ...

Lots of women had their hair cut short.

This is called a 'bob'.

In the 1970s ...

Both men and women had long hair.

But only the men had beards too!

In the 1980s ...

Young people had punk hairstyles.

Older people did not like it!

Hair in the 1980s was **VERY** extreme!

Hairstyles today

Today, there are lots of different hairstyles around. Sometimes, new hairstyles are started by famous people.

Footballers can be just as famous for their hair as they are for their football skills!

Some people shave their hair off!
You can make patterns in short hair ...

... and you can make patterns in
long hair.

Hairstyles may change but one thing stays the same – no one likes to have a 'bad hair day'!

But if your hair doesn't look good you can always wear a hat!

Quiz

Text Detective

- What parts of your body do not have hair?
- Have you ever had a *'bad hair day'*?

Word Detective

- **Phonic Focus:** Adding 'ing' to verbs ending in 'e'
  Page 7: Which letter must be dropped from 'have'
  before adding 'ing'?
- Page 9: Find a word meaning 'hid'.
- Page 10: Find two smaller words in the word 'hairstyle'.

Super Speller

Read these words:

because   having   today

Now try to spell them!

HA! HA! HA!

Q A man went out in the rain
without an umbrella but not a hair
on his head got wet! How?

A He was bald!

15

Before Reading

In this story

 Ziggy

 Pod

 The hairdresser

Tricky words

- mission
- hairdresser's
- hairdryers
- machines
- Brain-Boost
- whispered
- scissors

Introduce these tricky words and help the reader when they come across them later!

Story starter

Ziggy and Pod are aliens. They have been sent to Earth to find out how humans live. This time their mission is to find out about the human brain. They go to a hairdresser's because they think the hairdryers are Brain-Boost machines.

Aliens at the Hairdresser's

Ziggy and Pod had dressed up
as humans.

"Our mission today is to find out
about the human brain," said Ziggy.

"OK, boss," said Pod.

Ziggy and Pod saw a hairdresser's shop.
They could see humans sitting under
big, round hairdryers.

"Those machines are just like the Brain-Boost machines at home. They will help us find out more about the human brain," said Ziggy.

The aliens went into the hairdresser's.

"Hello," said the hairdresser.

"Having a bad hair day, are you?"

Ziggy pointed at the hairdryers.

"We want to use those machines, please," he said.

"First you must have a wash and trim," said the hairdresser.

"What is she going to wash and trim?" whispered Pod.

"I think humans have to wash their brains before they use the Brain-Boost machines," said Ziggy.

"Good thinking, boss," said Pod.

Ziggy and Pod sat down.
The hairdresser began to wash
Ziggy's hair.
"What is she putting on your hair?"
said Pod.
"I don't know," said Ziggy,
"but it smells nice."

"Are you going away this year?"
asked the hairdresser.
"No," said Pod, "we're staying
on Earth."

The hairdresser picked up some scissors.

"What are you doing?" screamed Pod.

"I'm going to trim your hair," she said.

"No," said Pod. "It will hurt me."

"Don't be silly," said the hairdresser.

"It's only your hair."

"Shhhh!" whispered Ziggy to Pod.

"Humans must let hairdressers cut them."

Then he said to the hairdresser,

"You can cut my hair if you like."

The hairdresser cut their wigs. Ziggy and Pod were very scared. "Be brave," whispered Ziggy. "We must do what humans do before using Brain-Boost machines!"

When the hairdresser had finished,
Ziggy and Pod looked in a big mirror.
Their hair looked very different.
"Now you can use the hairdryers,"
said the hairdresser.
"At last! The Brain-Boost machines!"
whispered Ziggy.

The aliens sat under the hairdryers. The hairdresser switched the machines on. Ziggy and Pod screamed.

Have you ever seen hairdryers like these?

"What a noise!" cried Pod.

"And it's frying my brain!" cried Ziggy.

Ziggy and Pod ran out of the shop.
They ran all the way back to their
spaceship to write their mission report.
"No wonder human brains are so small,"
said Ziggy.

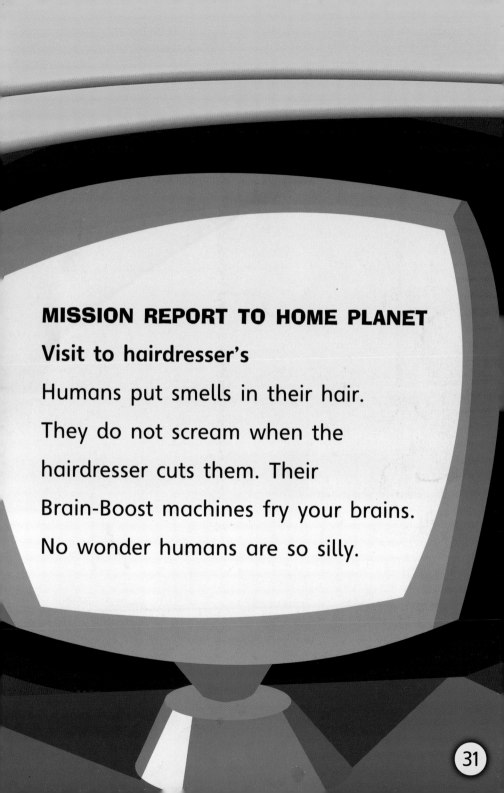

MISSION REPORT TO HOME PLANET

Visit to hairdresser's

Humans put smells in their hair.
They do not scream when the
hairdresser cuts them. Their
Brain-Boost machines fry your brains.
No wonder humans are so silly.

Quiz

Text Detective

- What did Ziggy and Pod think the hairdryers would do for humans?
- What part did you think was the funniest?

Word Detective

- **Phonic Focus:** Adding 'ing' to verbs ending in 'e'
  Page 30: Which letter must be dropped from 'write' before adding 'ing'?
- Page 20: Find a word meaning 'cut'.
- Page 24: Which punctuation mark ends the sentence starting with 'What'?

Super Speller

Read these words:

please   writing   before

Now try to spell them!

HA! HA! HA!

Q How does an alien count to 15?

A On its fingers.